FOREWORD

This is a story about friendship written by one of my very first friends, Amy Prideaux. Amy was a spunky girl who loved to dance and make people laugh. Even Amy's name was fun — Prideaux — a French name that rhymes with burrito. Amy and I grew up together, sharing school lockers, sharing laughs and sharing secrets. Whenever I think of her, it puts a smile on my face. I know Amy would want you to make lots of friends too with people who put a smile on your face and a pep in your step! **Being a friend to someone is one of the most important things you can do with your life. Special friendships will stay in your heart forever no matter where you are.**

Senator Janet Petersen
Iowa Senate

MANY THANKS TO:

Mrs. Johnson - Principal Capitol View Elementary School, Des Moines, Iowa
Teachers & Office Staff at Capitol View Elementary School, Des Moines, Iowa
Alicia VanAusdall - Owner/Art Director, Basilblue Design Company
All of the generous artists listed below.

The Artists	Relationship	Page	The Artists	Relationship	Page
Max	Friend, Grade 7	Cover	Donovan	Nephew	16
Jerome	Student, Grade 3	1	Dakota N.	Student, Grade 4	17
Kayla	Student, Grade 3	2	Lacey	Church Friend	18
Donald	Student, Grade 4	3	Jeanne	Church Friend	19
Ambrose	Student, Grade 4	4	Betty	Church Friend	20
Billie	Student, Grade 5	5	Sawyer	Church Friend, Pre K.	21
Spencer	Church Friend, Grade 2	6	Janet Prideaux	Mom	22
Duncan	Student, Grade 3	7	Ken Prideaux	Dad	23
Alex	Student, Grade 3	8	Tina	Cousin	24
Kalik	Student, Grade 4	9	Shelly	Sister	25
Jessica	Student, Grade 5	10	Jodi	Sister-in-law	26
Ashlea	Niece, Grade 8	11	Corey	Brother	27
Rachel	Niece, Grade 8	12	Todd	Brother	28
Trenton	Nephew, Grade 9	13	Anita	Colleague	29
Micah	Nephew	14	Tiffany	Colleague	30
Hannah	Niece, Grade 4	15	Kevin	Colleague	31

One sunny morning, on the Tanner's farm, a litter of piglets was born.

A very special piglet was in that litter.

Her name was Lisa Marie.

Jerome - Student, Grade 3

1

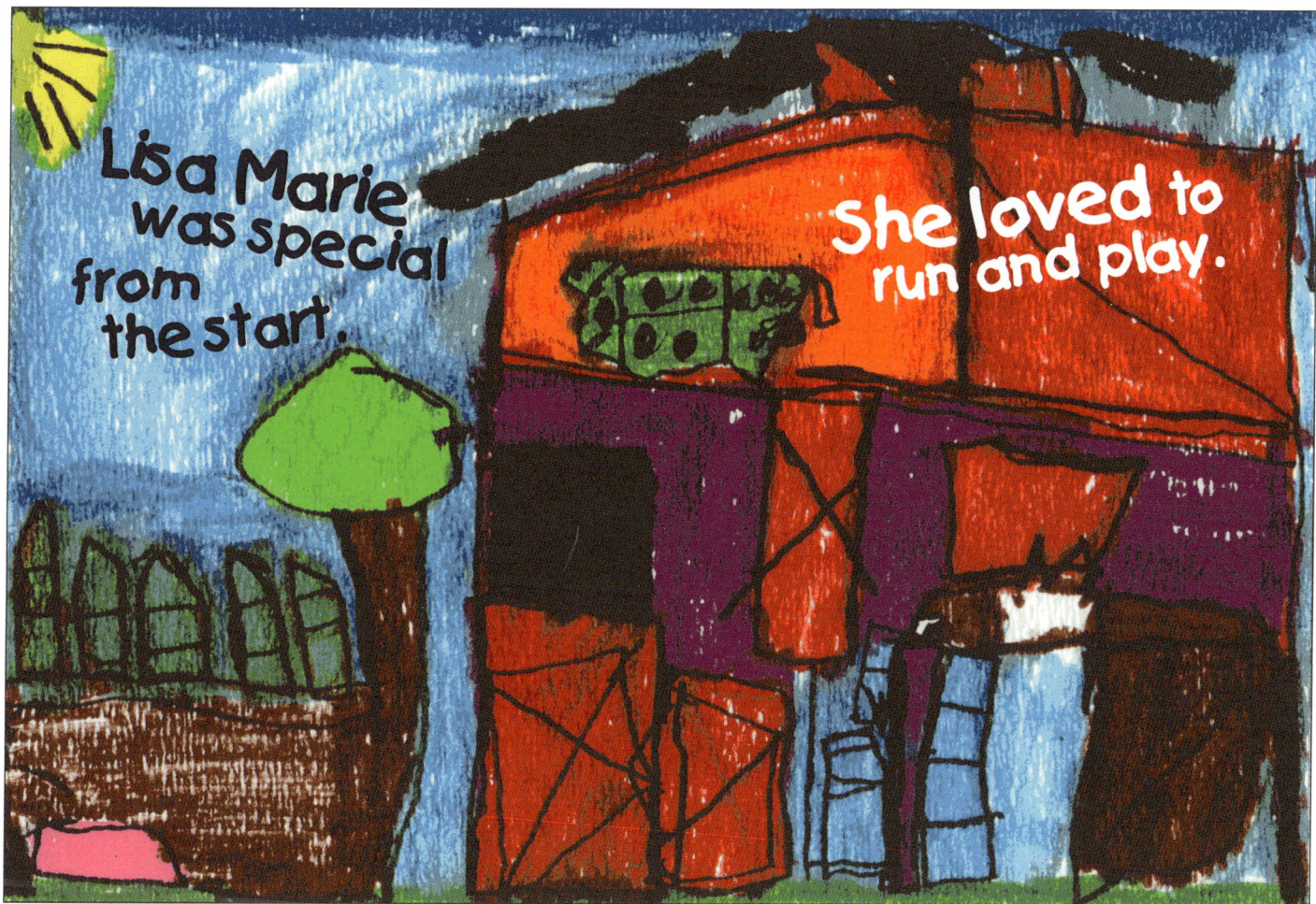

Kayla - Student, Grade 3

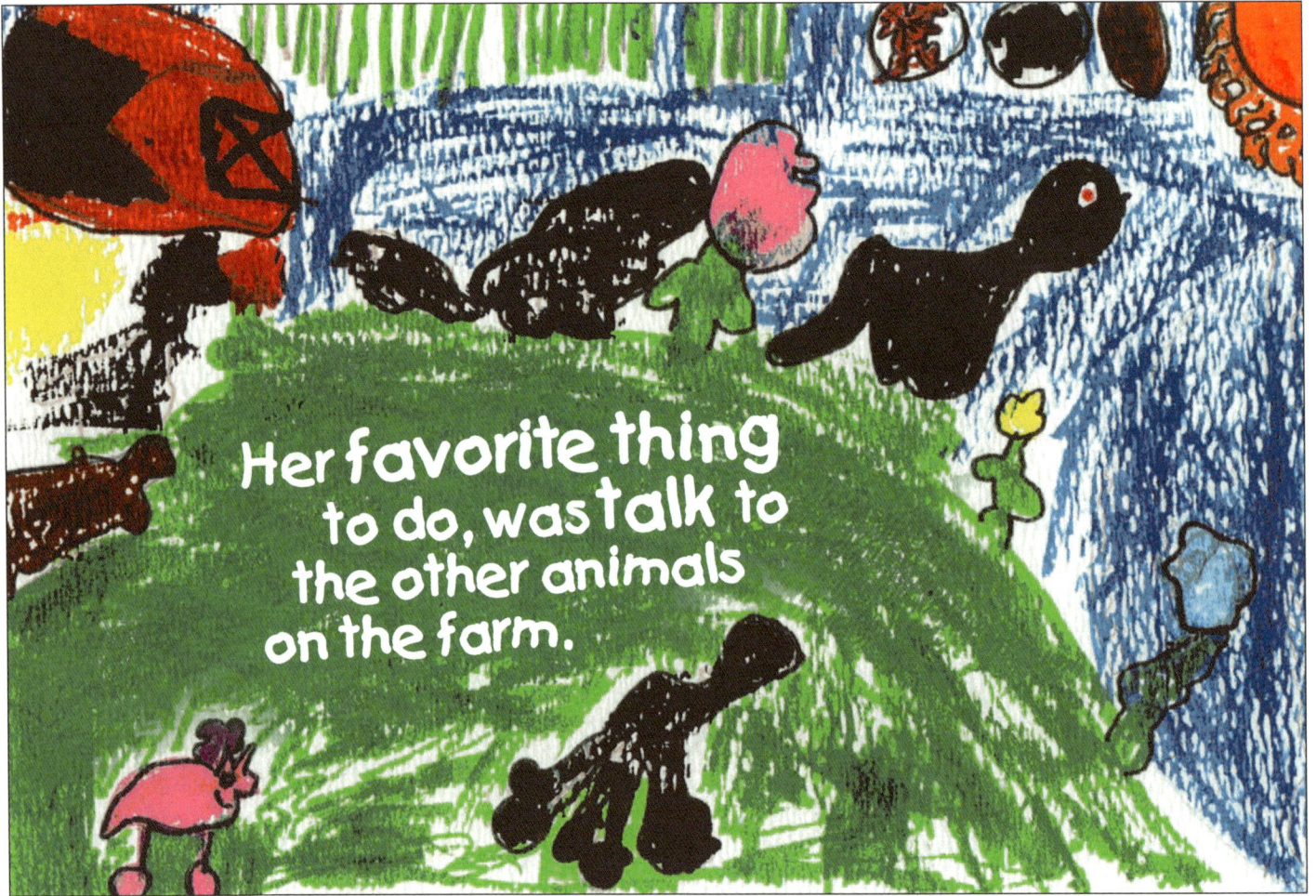

Her favorite thing to do, was talk to the other animals on the farm.

Donald - Student, Grade 4

Lisa Marie went to see her friends everyday.
She liked to go to the pond with her friend Sally, the lamb.

Ambrose - Student, Grade 4

It was also great fun
to run in the grass
with Brad,
the dog.

Billie - Student, Grade 5

Lisa Marie loved rolling in the mud with her friend Janet, the calf.

Lisa Marie was very happy on the farm.

Spencer - Church Friend, Grade 2

6

One day Lisa Marie was rolling in the mud when she saw something she had never seen before.

Duncan - Student, Grade 3

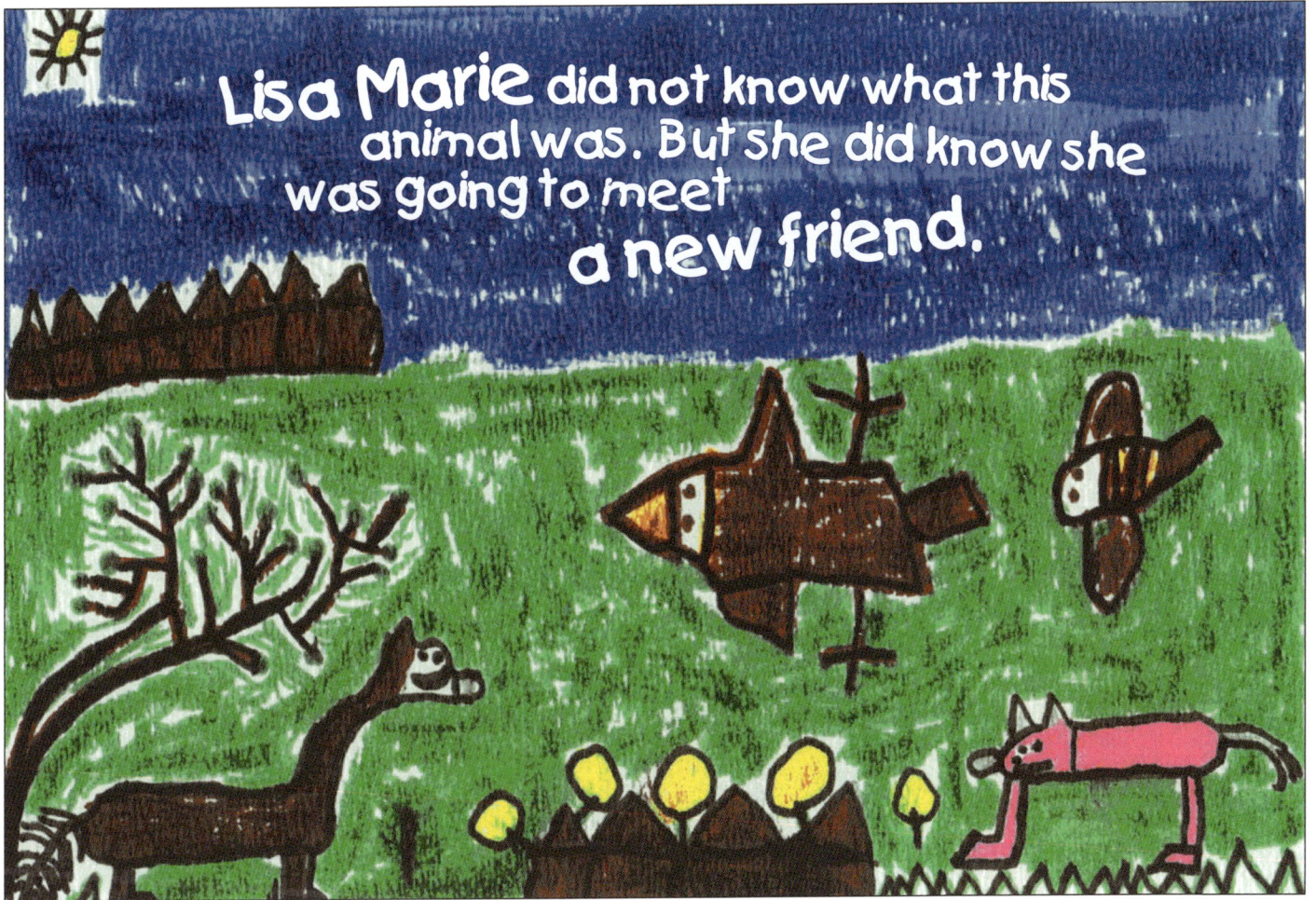

Lisa Marie did not know what this animal was. But she did know she was going to meet a new friend.

Alex - Student, Grade 3

Lisa Marie went over to the animal and said, "Hi. My name is Lisa Marie."

"Hi. My name is Glen.

I'm happy to meet you." said the strange new face.

Kalik - Student, Grade 4

9

"What kind of animal are you?" asked Lisa Marie. "I'm a llama." answered Glen. "It's nice to meet you." said Lisa Marie. "I've never met a Llama before."

Jessica - Student, Grade 5

Lisa Marie and Glen quickly became very good friends. They did everything together. The two animals liked helping their other friends.

Ashlea - Niece, Grade 8

11

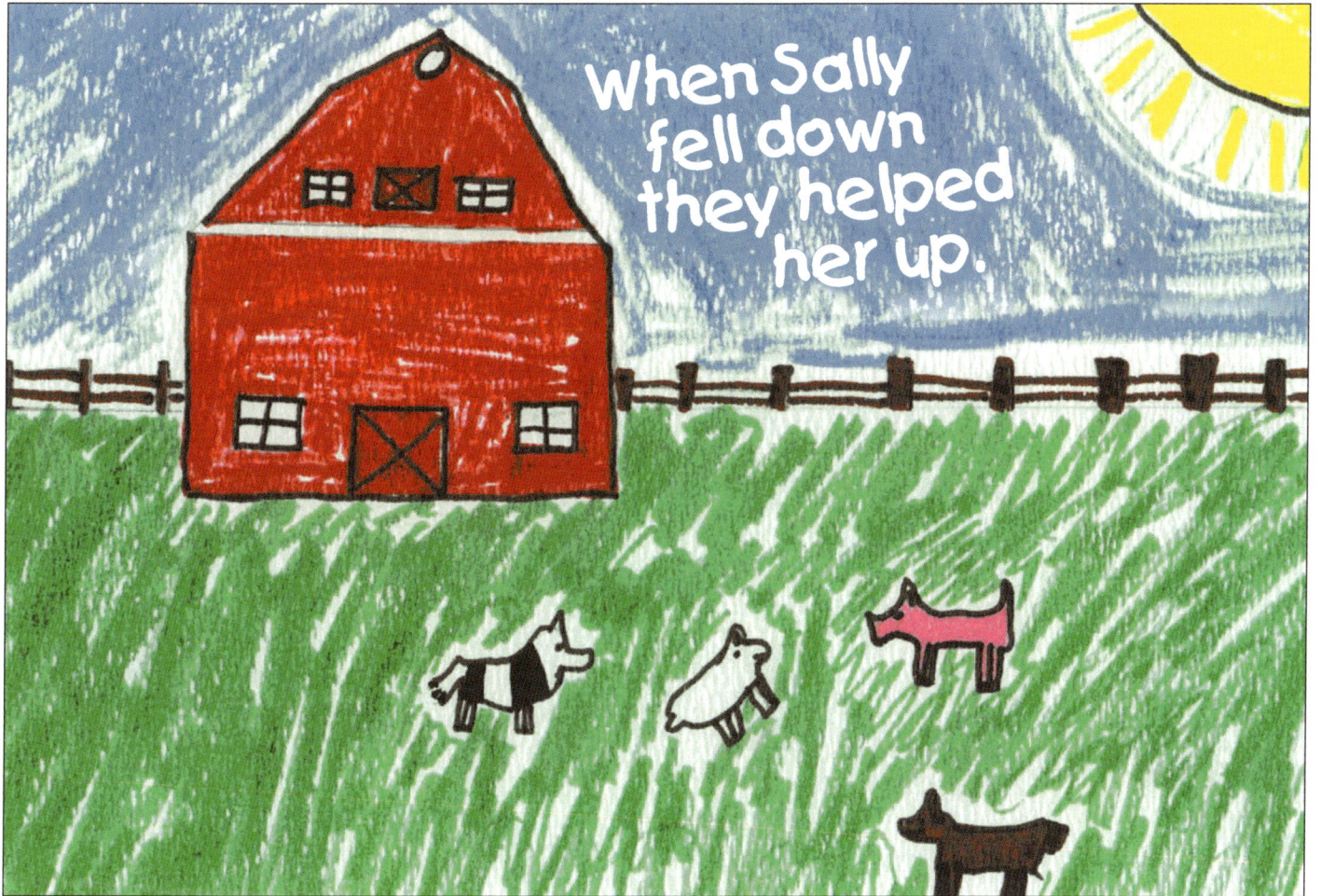

When Sally fell down they helped her up.

Rachel - Niece, Grade 8

When Brad had his feelings **hurt** they made him **feel better.**

Trenton - Nephew, Grade 9

Micah - Nephew

Hannah - Niece, Grade 4

Donovan - Nephew

Lisa Marie was very sad. Glen was her best friend.

She didn't want him to leave the farm.

Dakota N. - Student, Grade 4

Saturday morning came. Lisa Marie and Glen knew they had to say good-bye.

They met at the barn door. The two friends promised to never forget each other.

Lacey - Church Friend

Lisa Marie watched sadly as Bud loaded Glen into the trailer.

She turned to go to the mud hole as the trailer drove away.

Jeanne - Church Friend

19

Lisa Marie was too sad to play. She sat down in the grass and frowned.

Betty - Church Friend

The next day Brad asked Lisa Marie to run in the grass.

She was still too sad. She just sat and frowned.

Sawyer - Church Friend, Pre K.

21

Sally asked Lisa Marie to go to the pond.

But she was still too sad. She just sat and frowned.

Janet Prideaux - Mom

22

Farmer Tanner **noticed** that Lisa Marie was not playing with her other friends anymore. **He was worried** about her and thought she might be **missing** Glen.

Ken Prideaux - Dad

Farmer Tanner decided to take Lisa Marie for a visit with Glen. He loaded her into the truck and told her they were going to see a friend.

Lisa Marie was still sad but it was a beautiful day for a drive.

Tina - Cousin

Lisa Marie wondered where they could be going.

She watched out the window for a clue as the truck drove by the barn and then the pond.

Shelly - Sister

25

Farmer Tanner slowed to turn into the driveway of a farm. As they got closer, Lisa Marie noticed a pond and a barn. It was a red barn, like the barn she lived in.

Jodi - Sister-in-Law

The truck soon came to a stop.

Farmer Tanner lifted Lisa Marie out of the truck and led her behind the big red barn.

Corey - Brother

What a **beautiful day indeed!** Lisa Marie could not believe her eyes. **It was Glen.** The two friends were so excited to see each other.

They instantly **started** to play together, **just like old times.**

Todd - Brother

28

Anita - Colleague

Farmer Tanner came to take Lisa Marie home. He told her she could play with Glen again very soon.

She said good-bye to Glen and got into the truck.

Lisa Marie was very happy.

Tiffany - Colleague

As Lisa Marie rode home she thought about her day.

Kevin - Colleague

Lisa Marie thought...

How nice it was,
that even though Glen had moved away,
he was still her friend.

She started planning all the fun
they would have next time.

CRAFT

Make your own Lisa Marie using the template below.
Directions: Cut out each shape and assemble.
Color or decorate her any way you want.
For a curly tail, cut along the dotted line and
attach to the back side of the body at the "X".
Follow this drawing for reference when assembling. ➜

Mouth

Head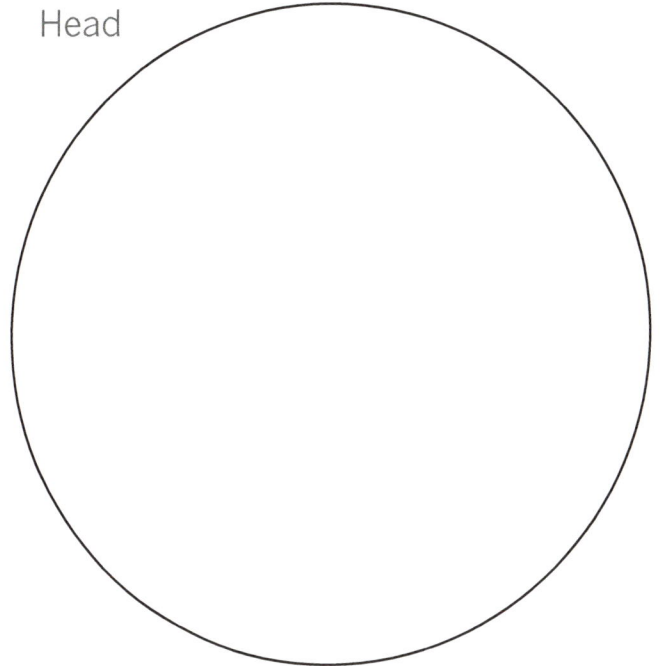

Tail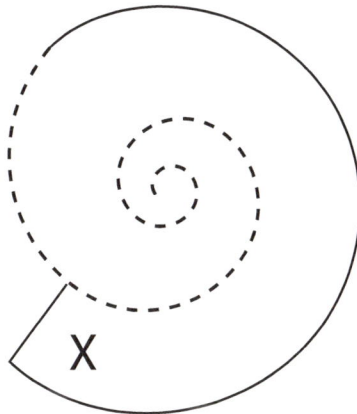

X

Feet

Ears

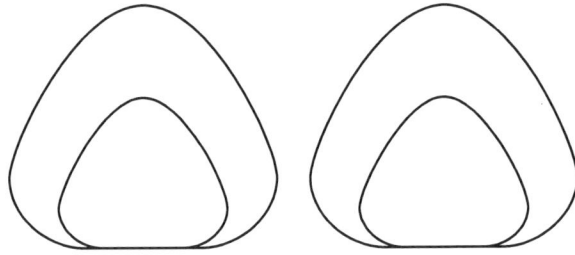

Snout

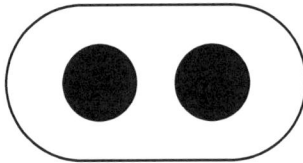

Eyes

Body

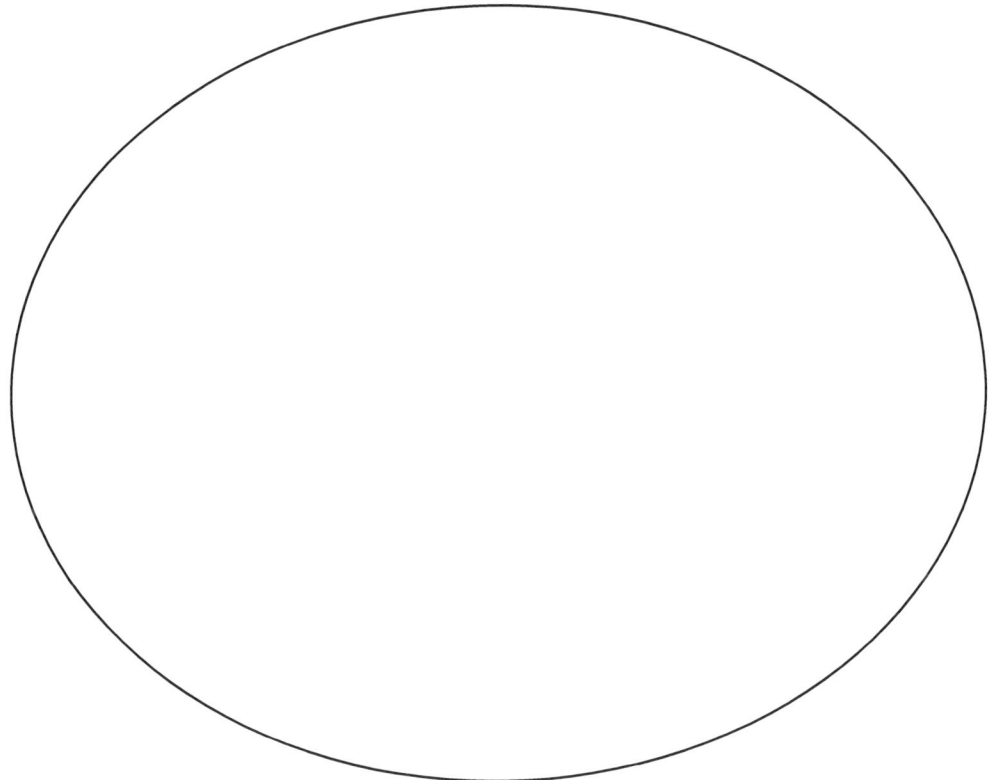

IN LOVING MEMORY

Amy was one of my dearest friends growing up through Junior High and High School. We were in cheerleading, drill team and music together in school and she invited me to join in her youth group at church. (Too many adventures to recount, but trust that they are filled with tons of laughter.) The rest of the time we spent on the phone or roaming about to make sure we didn't miss a beat. She was always creative when it came to the arts, music & dance and making our own fun. Amy was a huge impact on my life when I needed friends the most and was always there when I called. Our lives went in separate directions after high school, but we rekindled our friendship following college and moving back to Des Moines. Amy wrote this story and had shared the original draft with me to see what I thought about producing it. Not long after, she was tragically killed in a car accident. I held onto the story knowing that I needed to do something with it for her family. To my surprise, they knew of the story, as well, and called me about it. I told them I had the original draft and that started the ball rolling to get it produced to share with others. The illustrations were graciously drawn by her former students, friends and family members. It has been a long time coming, but with the help and patience of Janet and Ken (Amy's awesome parents), I have designed this book with Amy on my shoulder and in my ear, cheering the entire way. "You can do it if you try! V-I-C-T-O-R-Y!" It has been my honor to be a part of this project in memory of my dear friend. And to have witnessed first-hand her commitment and love for her "ba-zillions" of friends over the years. Ironically, I found a note from Amy (one of many we passed back and forth during grade school). She had always signed them "mon amie". Which in French means, "My Friend", of course.

Alicia VanAusdall

Owner / Art Director
Basilblue Design Company

19043195R00025

Made in the USA
Charleston, SC
04 May 2013